SOCCER CHAMPIONS

BY JIM WHITING

MANCHESTER UNITED

Published by Creative Education
and Creative Paperbacks
P.O. Box 227, Mankato, Minnesota 56002
Creative Education and Creative Paperbacks
are imprints of The Creative Company
www.thecreativecompany.us

Design and production by The Design Lab
Art direction by Rita Marshall
Printed in Malaysia

Photographs by Corbis (Matthew Ashton/AMA,
Colorsport, Lebrecht Music & Arts/Lebrecht Music &
Arts, KIMIMASA MAYAMA/epa, Mirrorpix/Splash
News, Phil Noble/Reuters, Phil Oldham/Colorsport,
DARREN STAPLES/Reuters), Getty Images (Popperfoto,
Bob Thomas), photosinbox.com, Shutterstock (AGIF,
gualtiero boffi, catwalker, Debu55y, Mitch Gunn, Denis
Kuvaev, Andy Lidstone, mooinblack, naipung, Jaggat
Rashidi), Wikimedia Creative Commons (Pbroks13)

Library of Congress Cataloging-in-Publication Data
Whiting, Jim.
Manchester United / by Jim Whiting.
p. cm. — (Soccer champions)
Includes bibliographical references and index.
Summary: A chronicle of the people, matches,
and world events that shaped the European
men's English soccer team known as Manchester
United, from its founding in 1878 to today.
ISBN 978-1-60818-589-4 (hardcover)
ISBN 978-1-62832-194-4 (pbk)
1. Manchester United (Soccer team)—History. I. Title.

GV943.6.M3W57 2015
796.334'640942733—dc23   2014029737

CCSS: RI.5.1, 2, 3, 8; RH.6-8.4, 5, 7

First Edition HC 9 8 7 6 5 4 3 2 1
First Edition PBK 9 8 7 6 5 4 3 2 1

Cover and page 3: Striker Wayne Rooney
Page 1: 2008 Champions League final

CONTENTS

Forward Danny Welbeck

INTRODUCTION

Soccer (or football, as it is known almost everywhere else in the world) is truly a universal game. Nowhere is the play more competitive than in Europe. Almost every European country has its own league, and generally that league has several divisions. A typical season lasts eight or nine months, from late summer to mid-spring. Every team in each level plays all other teams in its level twice, once at home and once on the other team's pitch. At the end of the season, the bottommost teams in one division are relegated (moved down) to the next lower division, with the same number of topmost teams from that lower division promoted to replace them. Such a system ensures that a high level of competition is maintained and that late-season games between teams with losing records remain important as they seek to avoid relegation.

Individual countries also feature their own tournaments, such as England's FA Cup and Spain's Copa del Rey. In theory, these tournaments allow almost any team the opportunity to win the championship, but in reality the best clubs dominate the competition. An assortment of European-wide tournaments complement individual nations' league and cup play. The most prestigious is the Union of European Football Associations (UEFA) Champions League. Known as the European Cup until

England's Manchester United became a championship football club, today counted among the world's greatest.

1993, the Champions League is a tournament consisting of 32 teams drawn primarily from the highest finishers in the strongest national leagues. Other teams can play their way into the tournament in preliminary rounds. It originated in 1954, when the otherwise obscure Wolverhampton Wanderers of England defeated Honved, the top-rated Hungarian side, prompting Wanderers manager Stan Cullis to declare his team "Champions of the World." Noted French soccer journalist Gabriel Hanot disagreed and helped organize a continent-wide competition that began in 1956.

The Champions League starts with eight four-team pools, which play two games with one another. The top two teams from each pool begin a series of knockout rounds, also contested on a two-game basis. The last two teams play a single championship game at a neutral site. The tournament runs concurrently with league play, beginning in September and concluding in May. Teams that win their league, their national cup, and the Champions League during the same season are said to have won the Continental Treble—almost certainly the most difficult feat in all of professional sports. The winner of the Champions League is eligible for the FIFA Club World Cup, an annual seven-team tournament that originated in 2000. It also includes teams from the Americas and Caribbean, Africa, Asia, Oceania, and the host nation.

The other major European club championship is the UEFA Europa League, founded in 1971 and known as the UEFA Cup until the 2009–10 season. The winners of these two tournaments play for the UEFA Super Cup, usually held in August.

ALL-TIME CHAMPIONS LEAGUE RECORDS OF THE TOP 10 CLUBS (AS OF 2014):

	Winner	Runner-up
Real Madrid (Spain)	10	3
AC Milan (Italy)	7	4
Bayern Munich (Germany)	5	5
Liverpool (England)	5	2
Barcelona (Spain)	4	3
Ajax (Netherlands)	4	2
Manchester United (England)	3	2
Inter Milan (Italy)	3	2
Benfica (Portugal)	2	5
Juventus (Italy)	2	5

Old Trafford stadium

CONTINENTAL TREBLE WINNERS

Celtic (Scotland)	1966–67
Ajax (Netherlands)	1971–72
PSV (Netherlands)	1987–88
Manchester United (England)	1998–99
Barcelona (Spain)	2008–09
Inter Milan (Italy)	2009–10
Bayern Munich (Germany)	2012–13

A DOG AND THE RED DEVILS

Busy cotton mills loomed over the city of Manchester in the late 1800s, employing immigrants and others.

After its Roman founding in A.D. 79, the small town of Manchester remained relatively untouched in northwestern England for more than 1,700 years. Then, early in the 19th century, thousands of people began pouring into the city for newly created factory jobs during the Industrial Revolution. Manchester soon became the largest industrial city in the world. Its most important industry was making textiles. With more than 100 cotton mills by 1853, the city earned the nickname "Cottonopolis." People even began calling cotton items such as sheets, pillowcases, and towels "manchesters"—a term still in use today. Eventually, the city's importance as an industrial hub declined.

Today, Manchester is an important financial center. It is further noted for its scientific research, music scene, and wide variety of media—such as television and newspapers—headquartered there. In addition, Mancunians, as the city's residents are termed, have long been treated to top-level soccer from two teams: Manchester City and especially Manchester United, which is one of the best known and most-followed teams of any sport in the world.

England is generally regarded as the birthplace of soccer, with records of the sport's ancestors dating back to the 1200s. The Football Association (FA) was formed in 1863 to oversee the sport and provide a uniform set of rules. Eight years later, it established the FA Cup, the world's first organized national soccer competition. All clubs that were members of the association were eligible to compete.

With that announcement, hundreds of teams began springing up, and Manchester was no exception. One of the city's new teams was the Newton Heath Lancashire and Yorkshire Railway Football Club, formed in 1878 by railroad

workers who wanted something to do on their free Saturday afternoons. They gave part of their pay to buy balls and uniforms.

As the team developed, two derbies—the name given to local or regional rivalries—quickly emerged. One was with crosstown rival Manchester City, founded in 1880 as St. Mark's (West Gorton) and taking on its present name 14 years later. The other—

regarded by many observers as perhaps the most intense derby in all of English soccer—was with Liverpool, a port city located about 40 miles to the west. Manchester needed to import raw materials (especially cotton) for its mills and, in turn, ship finished products to the world. The Liverpool and Manchester Railway opened in 1830 as Britain's first successful railroad and symbolized the interconnection between the two cities. However, Mancunians became upset with the increasingly high port charges that Liverpool levied. In 1894, they opened the Manchester Ship Canal, which allowed ships to sail directly to Manchester. Many Liverpudlians were outraged at the loss of income. The hostility between the two cities was—and still is—reflected on the soccer pitch in what became known as the Northwest Derby. "This is the game which rises above all others," said former Manchester coach Alex Ferguson, who retired in 2013. "You can't escape the history of a [Northwest Derby] and how much it means to the fans of each club."

Stephenson's Rocket *steam locomotive traveled the Liverpool and Manchester Railway.*

In 1888, the FA formed the Football League, pitting the country's top teams against each other. Four years later, Newton Heath (which had since dropped the railway part of its name) joined the league. It didn't do well at a higher level of competition and was relegated to the Second Division just two years later. Crowds dwindled, and by 1902, the club was on the verge of bankruptcy. Fortunately, wealthy brewery owner John Henry Davies

Newton Heath soccer players originally sported uniforms in the colors of green and gold and, later, blue and white.

and three other businessmen invested enough money to save the team. According to legend, a dog belonging to Newton Heath's captain Harry Stafford ran up to Davies at a club fundraiser. When Stafford retrieved his pet, the two men struck up a conversation about the team's plight, and Davies decided the club had enough potential for him to become involved. To reflect what was essentially a new start, a new name seemed appropriate. Newton Heath became Manchester United. To give the team a new on-field image as well, the uniform colors were changed from white and blue to white and red. The latter color gave rise to the team's nickname of "Red Devils."

UP AND DOWN— WAY DOWN

The team's fortunes began improving, and ManU (as people began to call it) finally rejoined the First Division in the 1906–07 season. A key contributor was halfback Charlie Roberts, considered by eventual Italian national team coach Vittorio Pozzo as the world's best soccer player. Roberts was also noted for wearing shorts that barely covered his thighs, unlike the common length that extended below the knees.

Under manager Ernest Mangnall (far left) and owner Davies (center), the 1907–08 Red Devils won the First Division.

After signing with ManU in 1906, Sandy Turnbull went on to tally 101 goals for the club.

ManU won its first league championship the following season, as Alexander "Sandy" Turnbull turned in 25 goals. Another key contributor was Billy Meredith, generally regarded as the team's first real star. The Red Devils went on to win the FA Cup in 1908–09.

These successes convinced Davies that the team deserved a better home field. Its current pitch was next to a marsh and often soggy, while nearby factories generated smoke and fumes. In 1909, Davies funded construction of the United Football Ground in a more upscale area of Manchester known as Trafford Park. It was part of a building boom that was transforming Manchester, and Davies spent lavishly to create what was regarded as the first modern soccer stadium in England, with room for 80,000 spectators. According to a contemporary journalist, "As a football ground, it is unrivaled in the world, [and] it is an honor to Manchester." Renamed Old Trafford in 1936, Davies's project has undergone several modernizations and is today universally regarded as one of the most hallowed stadiums in all of soccer.

Appropriately, the Red Devils scored the first-ever goal in their new facility. "[Right-half Dick] Duckworth took a free kick ... and skillfully dropped the ball some 10 yards or more from the goal-mouth," reported the *Manchester Guardian*. "A. Turnbull rushed in with lowered head. The ball was within a foot or two of the ground by the time he got it, but he met it with that extra-durable head of his and drove it hard into the goal." The score wouldn't stand up, though, as the Red Devils lost to archrival Liverpool 4–3.

ManU won another league title in 1910–11 before the outbreak of World War I in 1914 brought national-level soccer to a halt. Many soccer players answered the call to arms and were among the millions who perished during the next four years. When sporting events resumed in 1919, the long break proved unkind to ManU. The next two decades became known as "the years of depression," with the team mostly mired in the Second Division. The few spectators who turned out rattled around the stands. One of the few players to generate any excitement was Joe Spence. In 14 years with the club, the stocky winger scored 168 goals in 510 games. While he wasn't with the team as long, midfielder Frank Barson helped produce a rise in the team's fortunes in the mid-1920s—but only briefly.

The 1930–31 team was ManU's worst ever. It began the season with a 12-game losing streak and ended with 7 wins, 27 defeats, and 8 ties. Three years later, only a win in their last game of the season kept the Red Devils from tumbling out of the Second Division. A second-place finish in 1937–38 led to promotion the following season. That proved to be a stroke of good fortune when the onset of World War II led to the suspension of league play. When play resumed in 1946, the Red Devils remained in the First Division.

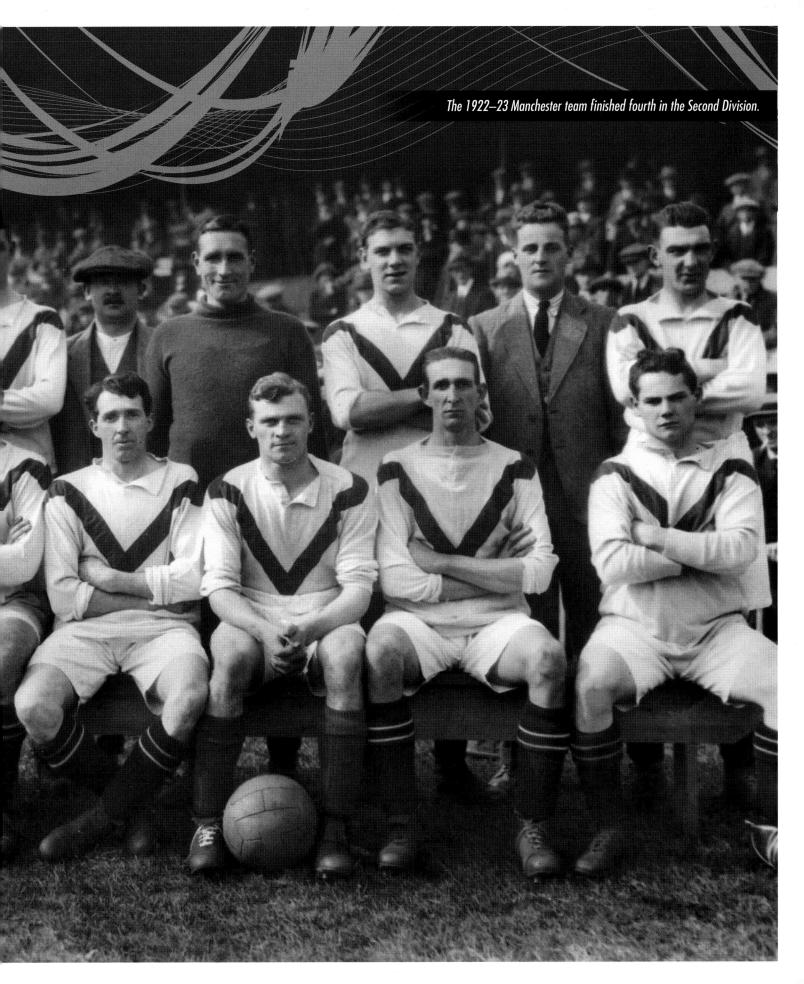

The 1922–23 Manchester team finished fourth in the Second Division.

"BUSBY BABES" ARE BORN

Under new manager Matt Busby, who had spent his entire playing career with ManU's two primary rivals, the team underwent an almost total turnaround from the dreadful interwar years. Led by fullback Johnny Carey (the team captain) and striker Jack "The Gunner" Rowley, the Red Devils finished just a point behind Liverpool in the 1946–47 season. They won the FA Cup in 1948, with Rowley—1 of only 4 ManU players to tally more than 200 goals in his career—scoring twice in a 4–2 victory over Blackpool.

At that time, it was customary for teams to buy established players from other teams. Busby chose a different strategy, launching a nationwide scouting program to identify promising young players and develop them. "If you're good enough, you're old enough," he explained. He even found a network of landladies who would look after the youngsters, many of whom were away from home for the first time. When the first two products of the system—midfielder Jackie Blanchflower and fullback Roger Byrne—made their debut in a game against Liverpool in November 1951, journalist Frank Nicklin coined the phrase "Busby Babes" to describe them. Several more players, such as halfback Duncan Edwards, forward David Pegg, and forward/midfielder Bobby Charlton—who would

Pioneering coach Matt Busby (above) believed in the potential of Bobby Charlton (opposite) and other Busby Babes.

be knighted for his contributions to soccer—arrived soon after. Though Manchester was the league's youngest team, Busby's gamble paid off. The team won back-to-back league championships in 1955–56 and 1956–57. Coupled with a runner-up finish in the 1957 FA Cup and reaching the semifinals of the European Cup in the same year, the Busby Babes appeared poised for greatness.

A day after winning a quarterfinal game in the European Cup to run their unbeaten streak to 11 matches, tragedy struck on February 6, 1958. A thick layer of slush on the runway at Munich-Riem Airport in Munich, Germany, prevented the plane carrying the team from generating enough speed to take off. Instead, the aircraft slammed into a house beyond the end of the runway. Twenty-three people were killed, including 8 players and 3 team officials, and 2 more players were injured so badly they would never play again. Busby was twice given the last rites

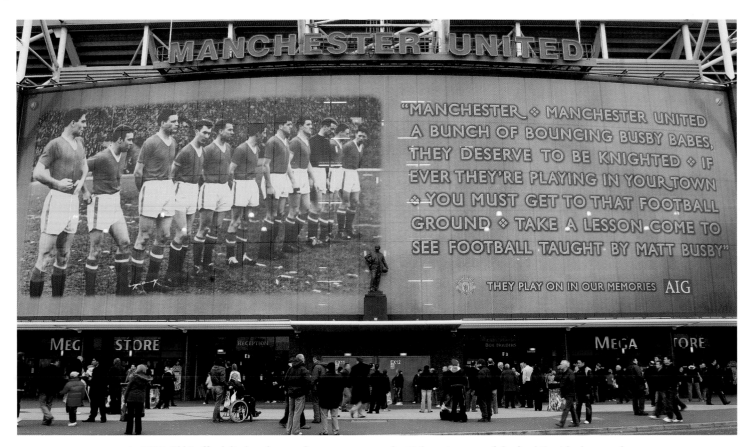

In 2008, Old Trafford displayed a mural to commemorate the 50th anniversary of the fatal Munich plane crash.

and expected to die soon after the accident. Later, he became so depressed that he wanted to quit, but his wife talked him into continuing with the club.

ManU carried on, with a mixture of reserves and players signed hastily from other teams. The team made the FA Cup finals and European Cup semifinals that year. Following a second-place finish in the 1958–59 season, the Red Devils dropped steadily in the standings until rebounding in 1962–63. New center-forward Denis Law joined with Charlton and forward George Best to give ManU its best team since the Munich disaster. The club won the 1963 FA Cup as Law scored six goals in six games. The success continued as the Red Devils were first or second in the league in four of the next five seasons and won England's first European Cup in 1968.

Busby retired the following year, and the effects were immediately obvious. By this time, the Busby Babes who had survived Munich had become soccer "senior citizens," and they began retiring as well. After three 8th-place finishes from 1969 to 1972, the Red Devils fell to 18th in the 1972–73 season. When the club tumbled to 21st in the following season, it was relegated. Adding insult to injury, the game that ensured relegation—the second-to-last of the season—was a 1–0 home loss to Manchester City. Even worse, the City score came from Denis Law, who had been discarded before the start of the season after 11 brilliant seasons with United. ManU responded by winning Second Division and was promoted back to First Division, where it has remained at the highest level of English soccer.

For the next 17 years, Manchester was a good but not great team, placing second in 1979–80 and 1987–88, and then dipping to 11th in 1988–89 and 13th in 1989–90. The Red Devils, however, did win the FA Cup four times in a little more than a decade. Their 1989–90 Cup was the first major accomplishment under manager Alex Ferguson, who had taken over during the 1986–87 season.

A statue of Best, Law, and Charlton ("The United Trinity") stands outside Old Trafford.

THE PREMIER TEAM IN THE PREMIER LEAGUE

The year 1992 was especially significant for both ManU and English soccer overall. In April, the Red Devils won the League Cup for the first time. Established in 1960, the League Cup is a knockout tournament involving the 92 teams at the top levels of English football, though it isn't as prestigious as the FA Cup. Forward Brian McClair scored the game's only goal, with an assist from midfielder Ryan Giggs. The teenaged

ManU's Brian McClair (second from left) celebrated his winning goal during the 1992 League Cup final.

As Ryan Giggs continued honing his skills, he made big plays happen by taking on more of a leadership role.

Giggs went on to win the Young Player of the Year award for 1992, the first of many honors that would eventually make him the most decorated player in English soccer history. At the time of the League Cup win, ManU was also leading the league and seemingly en route to its first title since the 1966–67 season. But three straight losses in late April allowed Leeds, unbeaten in its final five games, to claim the crown.

By then, a major change in English soccer was about to get underway. Driven by the prospect of a lucrative television deal, the 22 teams in the First Division broke away from the Football League and formed the Premier League. The new league still maintained links with the Football League through the system of relegation and promotion. But the extra money available to Premier League teams provided even more incentive for the bottommost teams to play hard and avoid relegation. Though

Alex Ferguson (foreground) and his "fledglings" won the 1999 Champions League.

ManU had the dubious distinction of giving up the league's first goal and losing during the opening-weekend matches, it won the 1992–93 title—its first league title in 26 years—by 10 points and a whopping 36-goal differential. The goal differential increased to 42 the following season as ManU easily won again.

Like his great predecessor Busby, Ferguson developed young talent and felt fully confident in players' abilities. When several veterans left after the 1994–95 season, Ferguson was harshly criticized for bringing up young players to replace them rather than buying established stars. The youngsters were immediately christened "Fergie's Fledglings" and included players such as midfielder Nicky Butt and defender brothers Gary and Phil Neville. The most famous fledgling was David Beckham, who would twice finish second in FIFA World Player of the Year voting (1999 and 2001). The up-and-comers' success justified Ferguson's faith, either winning Premier League championships or finishing near the top each year.

In 2003, the team signed the teenage Portuguese sensation and winger Cristiano Ronaldo. He requested number 28, the number with which he had begun his professional career. But Ferguson gave him number 7, which Best,

Beckham, and several others had worn. "The famous shirt was an extra source of motivation," Ronaldo said. "I was forced to live up to such an honor."

The year 2008 marked several anniversaries for Manchester United, including the 100th commemmoration of its first league title and the 40th anniversary of the team's first European Cup. Ronaldo became ManU's first Ballon d'Or winner since George Best 40 years earlier. On a much more melancholy note, 2008 was also the 50th anniversary of the Munich air disaster. In a fitting tribute to all those who had come before, ManU won both the Premier League and Champions League, defeating league rival Chelsea in the final. Manchester capped the year with a 1–0 win over Ecuador's LDU Quito, becoming the first English team to take the FIFA Club World Cup. After the win, ManU came very close to becoming the first two-time winner of the Continental Treble. The Red Devils lost 1–0 at Old Trafford in the FA Cup quarterfinals to eventual winner Portsmouth on a penalty kick late in the game. *The Guardian* soccer writer Paolo Bandini noted that Manchester players "contrived to miss about 300 gilt-edged chances in the space of 5 minutes" against a team that had finished 30 points behind them during the Premier League season.

Manchester took the top spot in the Premier League again in 2008–09. Seeking to become the first team to defend the Champions League title since Italy's AC Milan in 1990, ManU took on FC Barcelona of Spain, which had enjoyed an almost meteoric rise in the past few years. Unfortunately for ManU, the game resulted in a different kind of "first": by winning 2–0, Barcelona became the first Spanish team to take the Continental Treble. Ronaldo himself was bound for Spain soon after the match, when ManU accepted an offer of $132 million from Real Madrid.

Keeper Edwin van der Sar was ManU's hero of the 2008 Champions League final.

THE FERGUSON ERA ENDS

Sir Bobby Charlton joined the Red Devils for their winners' parade after capturing the 2011 Premier League title.

Despite the loss of one of its star players, Manchester's run of success under the direction of Ferguson—who had been knighted by Queen Elizabeth II in 1999 for his services to the sport of soccer—continued. The team was second in the Premier League in 2009–10 and first in 2010–11. ManU nearly won the title again in 2011–12. Tied with Man City going into the last game, ManU defeated Sunderland 1–0 on striker Wayne Rooney's goal. Meanwhile, Man City was losing 2–1 to the Queens Park Rangers. With the Red Devils waiting on the field for a possible trophy presentation, City scored two minutes into stoppage time to tie the score of its game and notched the winning goal three minutes later. Since ManU and Man City both finished the season with 89 points, officials had to determine which team had the greater goal differential before declaring a league winner. Unfortunately for ManU fans, City whisked away the title—the first time the Premier League champion was determined in that manner.

Ferguson announced his retirement as ManU's longest-serving manager soon afterward, and the Red Devils gave him a suitable going-away present by winning yet another Premier League title in 2012–13. In Ferguson's final game, his team uncharacteristically gave up a 5–2 lead to West Brom in the last 10 minutes. The game ended in a 5–5 tie. Fittingly, though, the game set 2 records: it was Ferguson's 1,500th

In April 2013, Manchester secured its 20th league championship by defeating Aston Villa at Old Trafford.

match and the first Premier League match in which the teams shared 10 goals.

Manchester struggled in the 2013–14 season under new manager David Moyes, eventually finishing seventh. Moyes was fired a month before the end of the season, which marked the team's lowest finish in more than 15 years and kept it out of European competition. Ryan Giggs became interim player-manager.

With a new generation of young talent already making its mark, the team seemed likely to rebound quickly. One promising player was keeper David De Gea, who joined the team in 2011 and soon assumed the starting role. Another was defender Phil Jones, touted by many as a possible future captain. A third was midfielder Adnan Januzaj, who joined the team at the age of 16 and whom the official ManU website termed "a creative force, able to … carve out openings with dynamic wing-play." In the season's waning days, 18-year-old striker James Wilson made a sensational debut, scoring two goals. He

Teenager Adnan Januzaj scored four goals in his rookie season for ManU.

thereby became the first-ever Red Devil to score for the organization's Under-18, Under-19, and Under-21 squads in addition to first-team ManU in the same season.

In early 2014, the team added midfielder Juan Mata from Chelsea. "It gives everybody a lift," Giggs said of the signing. "We've played against him for the last three years and know the quality he has got." Longtime leader Giggs retired in May but remained as assistant manager to newly signed coach Louis van Gaal. Formerly the Dutch national team coach, van Gaal had helped other European powerhouses capture league, national, and international titles.

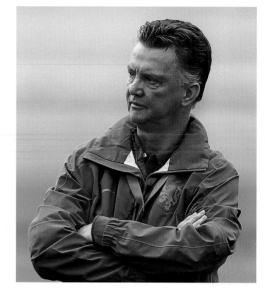

Louis van Gaal emphasized good technique, high confidence, and smart attacks.

One thing seems certain: the Northwest Derby will retain its intensity. Between 1972 and 1992, Liverpool won 11 First Division titles, while all other teams combined took 9, and ManU mustered only 3 second-place finishes. But the Red Devils turned the tables on Liverpool when the Premier League was formed, winning 13 titles between its 1992 establishment and 2013–14, with the other 9 going to practically every other team *except* Liverpool. The two clubs, therefore, have mirrored each other's success in English soccer for more than 40 years, and both claim superiority. In fact, the rivalry remains so heated that the last time a player transferred directly between the two clubs was in 1964. After the 2006–07 season, star ManU defender Gabriel Heinze demanded that he be allowed to go to

Juan Mata, a lethal goal-scorer, proved himself to be capable of important assists as well.

Liverpool. ManU fans who had chanted "Argentina!" in his honor then jeered him in retaliation. "We have received a written offer from Liverpool for Heinze," said ManU chief executive David Gill, "and we have rejected that, because it's Liverpool."

Whether they are playing derby rivals Liverpool or Manchester City, or taking on European foes such as Real Madrid or Bayern Munich, the Manchester United Red Devils can count on worldwide attention. According to *Forbes*, ManU was the world's third most valuable sports franchise in 2014 (behind Real Madrid and Barcelona), with a value of $2.8 billion and more than 650 million fans around the globe. The team had certainly come a long way from its origins, when railroad workers dug into their pockets to pay their expenses. ManU fans hoped that the team would soon resume what they regard as its rightful place in the upper reaches of the Premier League.

ManU's loyal fans reside in regions around the world, including Malaysia (pictured).

MEMORABLE MATCHES

1878

Team was founded.

1909

Manchester United v. Bristol City
FA Cup Final, April 24, 1909, London, England

In 1909, Manchester United and Bristol City were each making their first appearance in the finals. Despite suffering from a painful knee injury that limited his mobility, top scorer Alexander "Sandy" Turnbull begged to play. "Let him play," team captain Charlie Roberts told manager Ernest Mangnall. "He might get a goal, and if he does, we can afford to carry him." Roberts proved to be a prophet. "[Manchester forward Harold] Halse got the ball and kicked hard for the net," noted a *Manchester Guardian* sportswriter. "But the ball was a couple of inches too high and hit the underside of the crossbar. It rebounded toward A. Turnbull, who, with toe kept well down, sent in a sharp 'grounder' quite beyond the reach of Clay [in the Bristol City goal]." Coming midway through the first half, Turnbull's thrilling goal was the game's only score. In 2009, the Red Devils came close to winning the FA Cup on the 100th anniversary of their first win but fell in the semifinals on penalty kicks.

1968

Manchester United v. Benfica

*European Cup Final,
May 29, 1968, London, England*

Ten years after the Munich air disaster, Manchester had clawed its way back to the top of European soccer. The club had what amounted to home-field advantage over two-time winner Benfica of Portugal, with the match being played at London's Wembley Stadium. "All of England hoped and expected us to win," said captain Bobby Charlton, a Munich survivor. Charlton opened the scoring early in the second half with a header into the net. It was such a rare play for Charlton that Benfica star Eusébio congratulated him. Benfica equaled the score with 10 minutes left and nearly pulled off the win in the waning moments on a Eusébio breakaway, but ManU keeper Alex Stepney made a spectacular save. Eusébio helped Stepney to his feet and applauded him. When the match went into extra time, ManU put the game away with a 3-goal barrage within 10 minutes: forward George Best scored when Benfica didn't clear Stepney's long kick, forward Brian Kidd celebrated his 19th birthday with a header, and Charlton added his second score. Charlton noted that the 4–1 triumph "was something for the players who weren't here."

1977

Manchester United v. Liverpool

*FA Cup Final,
May 21, 1977, London, England*

In 1977, Liverpool was bidding to become the first English club to win the Continental Treble. The team had already won the league title and would face Germany's Borussia Mönchengladbach in four days for the European Cup crown. Winning the FA Cup was essential. But the Red Devils had another source of motivation. They had lost the FA Cup final the previous year to lowly Southampton—sixth in the Second Division—in a shocking upset. It would be especially satisfying to redeem themselves and disappoint their biggest rival in the process. After a scoreless first half, forward Stuart Pearson put ManU ahead six minutes into the second half when he took a through ball, outran two defenders, and rocketed in a goal from the right side of the penalty area. Liverpool quickly responded. The game-winner came when ManU forward Lou Macari took a shot toward the left corner of the net. Even though the ball deflected off a ManU player's chest, it still looped into the right side of the goal for the crucial score. Twenty-two years later, ManU would achieve the Continental Treble it had denied Liverpool in 1977.

1999

Manchester United v. Bayern Munich

Champions League Final, May 26, 1999, Barcelona, Spain

Playing in its first finals match in 31 years, ManU hoped for the first-ever English Continental Treble. But Bayern Munich scored on an early penalty kick, and the lead held up through regulation time. With just three minutes of stoppage time, Bayern fans began lighting fireworks, officials festooned the trophy with Bayern ribbons, and UEFA president Lennart Johansson left his seat to congratulate the winners. When he emerged from the tunnel onto the field, Johansson found a confusing scene. "The winners [Bayern] are crying, and the losers are dancing," he said. There was a good reason for the seeming oddity. Early in stoppage time, ManU striker Teddy Sheringham knocked a rebound into the goal after a David Beckham corner kick. Less than two minutes later, forward Ole Gunnar Solskjaer poked another Beckham corner kick into the roof of the net. "It was a two minute miracle you will tell your grandchildren about," wrote Jonathan Margolis of the *Daily Mail*. "The final 120 seconds of the 1999 European Cup final in Barcelona were simply the most breathtaking in sporting history."

2008

Manchester United v. Chelsea
Champions League Final,
May 21, 2008, Moscow, Russia

ManU seemed destined to win the first all-English Champions League final. The year 2008 marked anniversaries of the team's first league championship, its first European Cup title—and the Munich air disaster. Winger Cristiano Ronaldo gave ManU the lead midway through the first half of the final match, heading a cross by defender Wes Brown past keeper Petr Čech from about 12 yards out. Chelsea brought the score even just before halftime. When the teams were scoreless through overtime, the game went to penalty kicks. Ronaldo's uncharacteristic miss put Chelsea ahead by one. Chelsea captain John Terry lined up for the last kick, which would give his team the title. But Terry lost his footing and fell to the pitch just as he struck the ball, and it sailed wide.

In sudden death, keeper Edwin van der Sar poked away Nicolas Anelka's shot to give ManU the win. "Maybe it was fate, him missing his kick like that," said manager Alex Ferguson. "With the history of this club, we deserved to get this trophy tonight. I said that we wouldn't let down the memory of the Busby Babes."

2009

Manchester United v. Manchester City
Manchester Derby, September 20, 2009, Old Trafford, Manchester

An early-season derby became "a game that had everything—except for competent defending," according to BBC Sport football writer Phil McNulty. Though striker Wayne Rooney scored two minutes into the game, Gareth Barry soon brought City even. Midfielder Darren Fletcher's header just after halftime put ManU ahead again, but Craig Bellamy's booming 25-yarder retied the game 3 minutes later. Another Fletcher header with 10 minutes left appeared to seal the victory. But according to McNulty, a ManU defender "committed an error that would have shamed a schoolboy" by failing to clear the ball deep in the ManU end. Bellamy took advantage of the miscue to slam home the tying goal moments before the end of regulation time. With stoppage time running out, Red Devils striker Michael Owen took a pass to the left of the goal and barely beat a sliding defender and the keeper to win the game. "To score a goal as dramatic as that in a derby was amazing," he said. Manager Alex Ferguson immediately labeled the derby the best ever. In 2012, fans named it the best match in the league's 20-year history.

FAMOUS FOOTBALLERS

BILLY MEREDITH

(1874–1958)
Outside forward, 1906–21

Nicknamed the "Welsh Wizard," Billy Meredith is widely considered one of the earliest English soccer superstars. He made his debut at the age of 18 for his local team and joined Manchester City 2 years later. He led City in scoring his second year and was named team captain. In 1906, he moved to ManU and soon formed the foundation of a powerful front line. "His winding runs down the wing coupled with his pinpoint crosses made him an exceptional talent and one of the most popular footballers of his generation," notes the official Manchester United website. Often, Meredith would be marked by two, three, or even four opposition players, but he had an uncanny ability to find teammates who were left open as a result. In 1921, he became ManU's oldest-ever player at the age of 46 in a game against Derby County. Soon afterward, he returned to Man City and played there until he was nearly 50. Many people credit Meredith's longevity to the strength he gained as a coal miner during his teenage years and—unlike many other players of his era—not using alcohol or tobacco.

FRANK BARSON

(1891–1968)
Halfback, 1922–28

It was appropriate that Frank Barson began his working life as a blacksmith, because he was tough as nails. After beginning his football career with Barnsley in 1911, Barson displayed what would become his trademark brand of honesty. When he or a teammate was fouled, he would retaliate—after first telling the referee exactly what he planned to do. As a result, "on frequent occasions, Barson was escorted out of grounds by policemen to protect him from groups of angry opposition fans," the *London Times* reported. With ManU mired in the Second Division after World War I, team officials felt Barson could provide the energy and leadership they needed and persuaded him to come over from Aston Villa, his club at the time. They promised him his own pub if the team returned to the First Division within three years. As the *Manchester Guardian* noted, Barson "set the example of bold tackling, well-judged passing, and not a little daring that was of incalculable value."

ManU returned to the First Division, but Barson quickly realized that pub ownership wasn't for him. He gave the establishment to his head waiter and never returned.

DUNCAN EDWARDS

(1936–58)
Halfback, 1953–58

Duncan Edwards attracted the interest of ManU scouts when he was only 11 and signed his first contract four years later. Termed "a boy in a man's body," he became the youngest-ever First Division player in his 1953 debut as a "Busby Babe." He soon became a fixture in the ManU starting lineup, playing a key role in the team's championship seasons of 1955–56 and 1956–57. He also joined the English national team in 1955, and many people expected him to be a vital part of the 1958 English World Cup team. Sadly, Edwards never had the chance to play for that team. He suffered severe injuries in the Munich crash and died 15 days later. In an unfortunate coincidence, a soccer magazine with Edwards's photo on the cover was released just before his death. According to fellow Busby Babe Bobby Charlton, Edwards was "the only player that made me feel inferior." Longtime player and ManU manager Tommy Docherty added, "There is no doubt in my mind that Duncan would have become the greatest player ever. Not just in British football … but the best in the world."

GEORGE BEST

(1946–2005)
Forward, 1963–74

In 1961, ManU scout Bob Bishop could barely contain his excitement, telling manager Matt Busby, "I think I've found you a genius!" That "genius" was George Best, a teenager from Northern Ireland who made his debut in 1963 at just 17 years old. He scored the first of his 179 goals with the Red Devils the following game. Five years later, Best led the team in scoring and maintained that distinction for the next four seasons. His personal appearance drew comparisons with the most famous Englishmen of the era. When Best scored two goals to help ManU crush Benfica 5–1 in the 1965–66 European Cup quarterfinals, a Portuguese newspaper called him "El Beatle" because of his long hair. The English press quickly dubbed him the "Fifth Beatle." As Best explained, "I was 19 or 20 when The Beatles were at their peak, and I was coming up to the peak of my career, too. I was also the first footballer to have long hair." He became renowned for his partying lifestyle, which eventually affected his playing. Nonetheless, the famous Brazilian soccer player Pelé called Best "the greatest player in the world."

DAVID BECKHAM

(1975–)
Midfielder, 1992–2003

David Beckham burst onto the world soccer scene in 1996 when he blasted a shot from midfield in a game against Wimbledon that soared over the keeper's head and into the goal. That moment has become one of the most-replayed of all time. But it was just the beginning for Beckham, who had played his first game for the Red Devils when he was barely 17. He became a regular in 1995–96 and helped ManU win six league titles, two FA Cups, and a Champions League title. He especially relished being on the big stage, as many of his finest moments came with the English national team. He left ManU after the 2002–03 season for Real Madrid, where he played four seasons. Then he joined the Los Angeles Galaxy of Major League Soccer. Even though he retired in 2013, Beckham still maintains a high public profile. His marriage to former Spice Girl Victoria Adams made him an immediate celebrity. He often appears in commercials for clothing and other products. He is also noted for his work with charities such as UNICEF and Malaria No More UK.

RYAN GIGGS

(1973–)
Midfielder, 1991–2014
Assistant manager, 2014–present

Schoolboy soccer sensation Ryan Giggs had a surprise guest at his 14th birthday party: ManU coach Alex Ferguson. Giggs was enrolled in Man City's School of Excellence, but Ferguson gave him the promise of turning professional in three years. Giggs made his ManU debut late in 1990–91. The following season, he moved into the starting lineup—at just 17 years old—and remained there until his retirement. His rise coincided with that of ManU as the dominant Premier League team. "He is one of those special and rare players," said former ManU assistant manager Carlos Queiroz. "Side by side with his fantastic skills, he is a player with intelligence. It seems he is able to make others play better around him." In 2011, a worldwide poll conducted by ManU voted Giggs the team's greatest-ever player. ManU's Champions League triumph on May 21, 2008, marked Giggs's 759th match in a Red Devils jersey, breaking Bobby Charlton's record of 758. At the end of the 2013–14 season, the 40-year-old Giggs announced his retirement from playing but stayed on as assistant manager.

MANCHESTER UNITED TITLES
THROUGH 2014

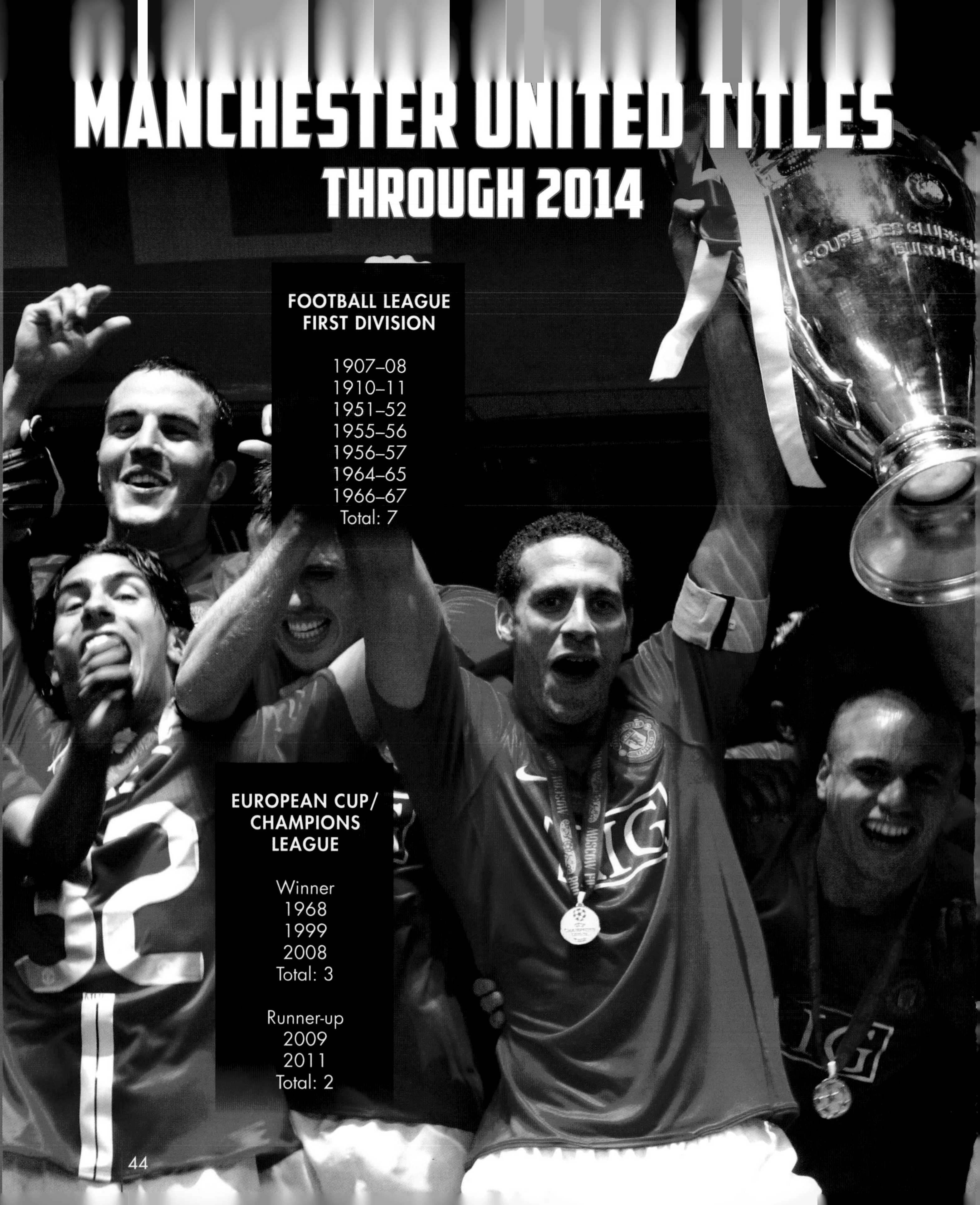

FOOTBALL LEAGUE FIRST DIVISION

1907–08
1910–11
1951–52
1955–56
1956–57
1964–65
1966–67
Total: 7

EUROPEAN CUP/ CHAMPIONS LEAGUE

Winner
1968
1999
2008
Total: 3

Runner-up
2009
2011
Total: 2

FA CUP

1908–09
1947–48
1962–63
1976–77
1982–83
1984–85
1989–90
1993–94
1995–96
1998–99
2003–04
Total: 11

LEAGUE CUP

1992
2006
2009
2010
Total: 4

PREMIER LEAGUE

1992–93
1993–94
1995–96
1996–97
1998–99
1999–2000
2000–01
2002–03
2006–07
2007–08
2008–09
2010–11
2012–13
Total: 13

SELECTED BIBLIOGRAPHY

Marshall, Ian. *Old Trafford: The Official Story of the Home of Manchester United.* London: Simon & Schuster, 2010.

Murphy, Alex. *The Official Illustrated History of Manchester United: The Full Story and Complete Record 1878–2006.* London: Orion, 2006.

Tyldesley, Clive, and Craig South. *Manchester United: Official History, 1878–2002.* DVD. Pleasanton, Calif.: Soccer Learning Systems, 2002.

UEFA. *Champions of Europe, 1955–2005: 50 Years of the World's Greatest Club Football; The Best Goals from All 50 Finals.* DVD. Pleasanton, Calif.: Soccer Learning Systems, 2005.

White, Jim. *Manchester United: The Biography, From Newton Heath to Moscow, the Complete Story of the World's Greatest Football Club.* London: Sphere, 2009.

WEBSITES

MANCHESTER UNITED
http://www.manutd.com/
The official Manchester United website, with information on current team members, biographies of past stars, up-to-date information about the current season, and much more.

PREMIER LEAGUE
http://www.premierleague.com/en-gb.html
The official Premier League website, with upcoming games, extensive news and features, standings, game and player photos, videos, and more.

Note: Every effort has been made to ensure that the websites listed above are suitable for children, that they have educational value, and that they contain no inappropriate material. However, because of the nature of the Internet, it is impossible to guarantee that these sites will remain active indefinitely or that their contents will not be altered.

INDEX